I ♥ RANCH
DRESSING

I ♥ Ranch Dressing

And Other Stuff White Midwesterners Like

C. L. Freie

Andrews McMeel Publishing, LLC
Kansas City

 For information, write Andrews McMeel Publishing, LLC, an Andrews McMeel Universal company, 1130 Walnut Street, Kansas City, Missouri 64106.

08 09 10 11 12 BSF 10 9 8 7 6 5 4 3 2 1

ISBN-13: 978-0-7407-7953-4
ISBN-10: 0-7407-7953-2

Library of Congress Control Number: 2008929312

www.andrewsmcmeel.com

For everyone I ♥,
especially my dad.

Your Standard Disclaimer:

Obviously, given the content, the use of various trademarks in this book does not constitute or suggest sponsorship, endorsement, or authorization by the owners of the trademarks pictured or referred to in the pages to follow.

I
RANCH
DRESSING

1. RANCH DRESSING

Jesus, Mary, and Joseph, ever since the ubiquitous ranch dressing landed on the scene, White Midwesterners have been putting this nectar of the gods on nearly everything. Pizza, burgers, fish sticks (guilty as charged), hot dogs—you name it, ranch dressing goes with whatever artery-clogging meal you rest on your fat thighs while watching TV.

Bob Evans
RESTAURANT
5870

2. BOB EVANS

I don't care who you are, if you are from anywhere in the central U.S. of A., your wider-than-normal tush has been into a Bob Evans. Heck, even the name of the place sounds like the guy who sells you auto insurance. Bob Evans is also super handy. I kid you not, my little friends—this is actually on their Web site (www.bobevans.com):

> Bob Evans has provided a service to assist when traveling. Simply enter your "Starting Point" and "Ending Point." Then click "Show Directions." A map will be created showing directions which includes Bob Evans Restaurants along the way.

3. EASILY DISCERNIBLE LUGGAGE

That bright orange gift-with-purchase tote bag from your wife Julie Anne's last trip to the Clinique counter is perfectly acceptable travel gear to a White Midwesterner. Oh, and White Midwesterners are really antsy about "some clown swiping our luggage" at baggage claim, hence the multitude of baggage "customizations" we employ. (Full disclosure: My sturdy black Samsonite carry-on has two ID tags, blue nail polish on the bottom, and my initials written in gold marker in no fewer than six places. Oh, and some old ribbon left over from Christmas is affixed to the side handle.) If we see somebody with matching luggage, WMs instinctively think that the owner is either (a) from the coast or (b) a foreigner. Both of which make WMs just a little bit uncomfortable.

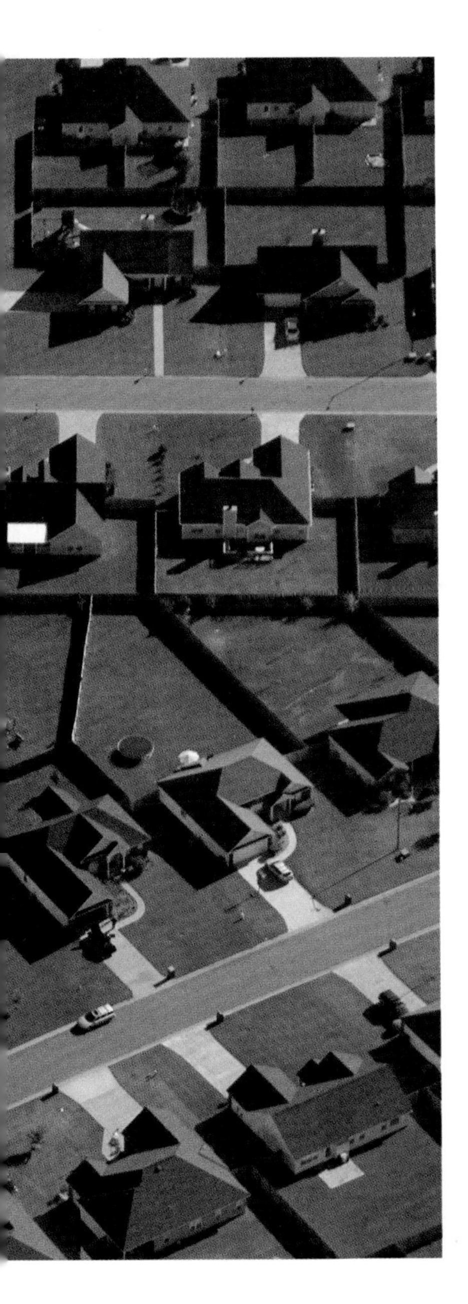

4. CUL-DE-SACS

White Midwesterners loooove cul-de-sacs. My ex-boyfriend, Ink, lives on a cul-de-sac and he's so proud. People who live on cul-de-sacs love to laugh at people who mistakenly go down their street, only to have to turn around in shame and go the other way. "Yeah right, you got the wrong street there, buddy. Heh."

5. “FOREIGN FOOD”

White Midwesterners love international travel (it makes us feel so worldly when we write our yearly Christmas letters), and we especially love to come back and carp about how bad the food was. Case in point: My friend Shannon and I were in Rome a couple of years ago and the food was ghastly—lots of gray meat and it tasted nothing like the Olive Garden. The fact is, we White Midwesterners love the idea of foreign food, but anybody will tell you that most of the Mexican restaurants here in town are “Taco Bell with a tablecloth” kinda joints and, frankly, we’re really OK with that. Real foreign food is usually made up of animals and vegetables that are completely, well, foreign to us, and that kinda grosses us out. A lot.

6. DOCKERS

Face it—a lifetime of Bob Evans breakfasts and ranch-dressing'd burgers make White Midwesterners a bit paunchy. No matter what the brand, Dockers are a staple of the White Midwesterner's wardrobe. Men love 'em, women love 'em. Nothing says "I've made it to middle management, buddy, so you should just stick to teaching my son's theater class and minding your own beeswax" like a sharply creased pair of pleated pants.

7. MAKEUP

As a White Midwestern chick, I can tell you that this category hits really close to home. I recently decided to go foundation-less on account of a weird rash and now I feel completely naked (and not in that good way when the lights are out). White Midwesterners completely lose their religion during Clinique Bonus Time. You'd think they were giving away healthy White babies instead of overpriced face paint, weird lipstick colors, and makeup bags that you–will–never–use.

8. NOVELTY SWEATERS

How better to say, “Flag Day is on its way!” than a lovely novelty sweater? Every young White Midwestern woman has had the joy of opening a birthday present from her mother-in-law that consists of a “hip” novelty sweater (with matching socks!). The cache of novelty sweaters is so strong that Internet sensation (and White Midwesterner) Leslie Hall became a YouTube star with her song about gem sweaters.

9. DIET CHERRY COKE

Did you know that Diet Cherry Coke was introduced in 1986 and renamed "Diet Coke Cherry" in 2005? This kind of information is important to White Midwesterners. White Midwesterners subsist on a diet of Applebee's and Stouffer's frozen lasagna, so when they're feeling a little frisky they'll break out the Diet Cherry Coke. It's just daring enough that they'll get a kick out of drinking it, but safe enough that if Pastor Bill from Macadamia Heights Family Church walks past on the way to the restroom it won't arouse too much suspicion.

10. COVERED-DISH SUPPERS

Around the lower Midwest we call them casseroles; up toward Wisconsin it's called a hotdish. Regardless, this is the signature "fancy" food of White Midwesterners. Going to a baptism? Bring a casserole. Belong to the Ladies Auxiliary at Macadamia Heights Christian Church and need to bring a funeral dish? Bring a casserole. The unifying factor among the various iterations of this culinary delight is the ubiquitous cream of mushroom soup, and the best ones have crunched-up potato chips on top (I know my mom's always did).

If you are new to the Midwest or—gasp—not White, you'd do yourself a favor to call up the nearest Missouri Synod Lutheran Church and purchase every edition of their yearly *Lord, That's Good!* cookbook. (Bonus points for every "salad" recipe therein that contains nothing beyond Jell-O, Cool Whip, and fruit cocktail.)

11. HUGE CHRISTIAN CHURCHES

White Midwesterners like things big—big McMansions, big-box retail stores, the comfort of big pants, and the safe, warm, enveloping atmosphere of the local megachurch. Megachurch pastors often brag that their churches are the size of the local "good mall" (read: no wandering punks). Another advantage of going to a megachurch is if you skip a week or two—or twelve—who will notice? While megachurches are usually some flavor of Protestant (though Catholics with our no-birthcontrollin' ways have always had big churches) there is one unifying characteristic: They are all predominantly White. *My Rod and my staff and my lack-of-diversity-among-parishioners, they comfort me.*

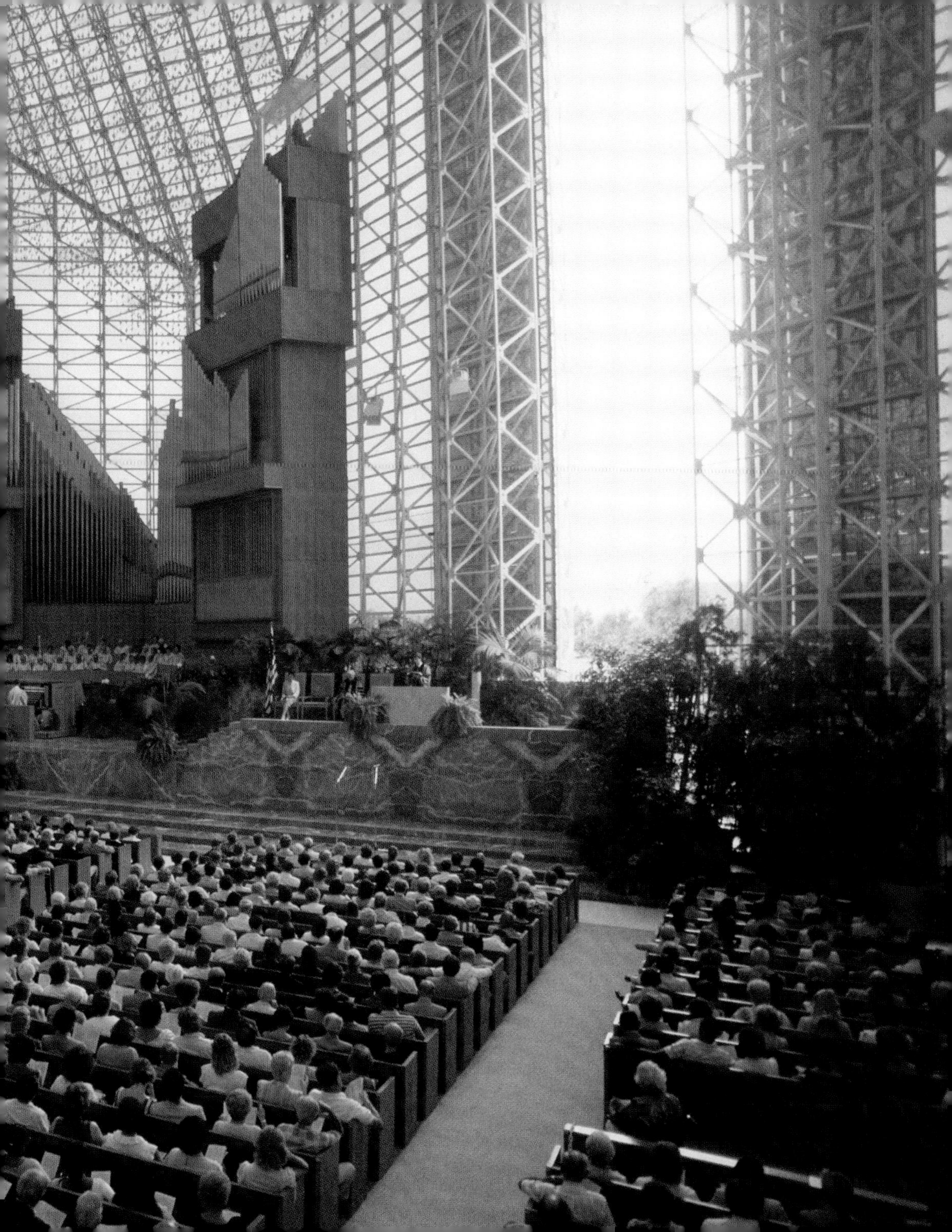

12. METH

OK, this is one White Midwestern thing that I'm not too proud of, but heck if every time you turn on the idiot box there isn't some show with a bunch of white folks making, doing, and/or selling meth. People actually brag about living in the meth capital of the U.S. And, whether we admit it to our WM selves or not, we all know somebody who did or does meth. (Here's a hint—that hot guy who does your hair? Who talks about his friend "Tina"? Probably doing meth. And your brother? Sorry.)

16. WHITE WICKER

Nothin' says, "Hey, I run a classy patio, Missy; we spell out our curse words" like a nice white wicker sofa. Next to a white wicker table. By a white wicker plant stand. And oh, wicker isn't *just* for the patio. White wicker will be found all over White Midwestern homes. Baby furniture? White wicker. Toilet paper holder? You guessed it. Apparently if we could make our entire homes out of white wicker we probably would. No other civilization would elevate such ridiculously impractical furniture to a status symbol.

17. CRAFT STORES

Well, where in the world did you think we *bought* our wicker furniture—Sears? Heck no, all things white wicker can be purchased at the local Midwestern craft store. White Midwestern women flock to craft stores the same way their husbands flock to half-price beer night at Hooters. Whether it is for cake decorating supplies, scrapbooking papers, or "the cutest John Deere fabric for our bedroom curtains," White Midwestern women can find it at their local Michael's or Hobby Lobby. Unless of course it's Sunday, because Hobby Lobby is closed for the Lord on Sundays.

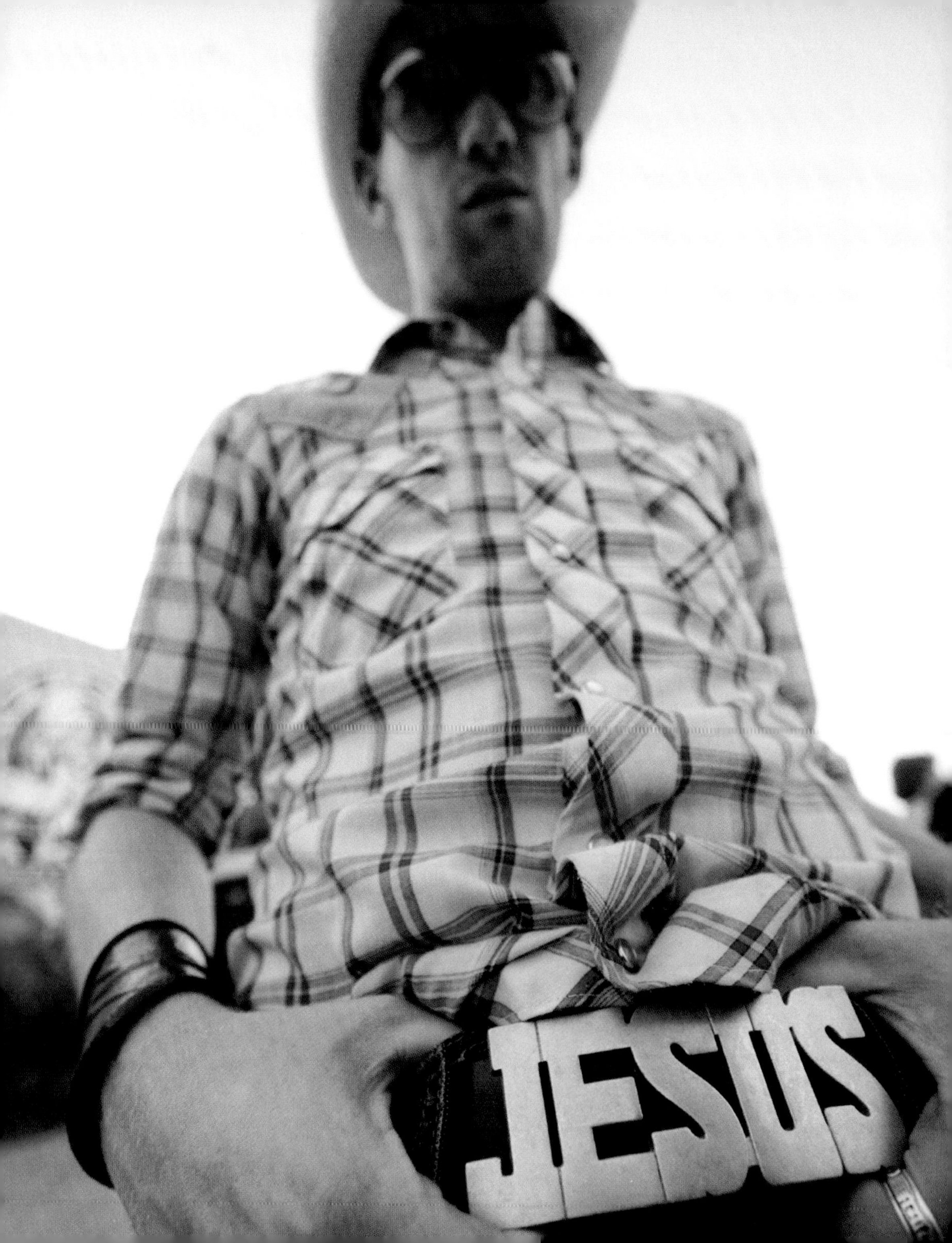
JESUS

18. JESUS

Oh, you betcha White Midwesterners love Jesus. We have Jesus in our hearts and on our sleeves. Our favorite Jesus is the one who is your child's special pal but who smites sinners with a fiery gusto, but there are other Jesuses available for your enjoyment. There is the "Plays soccer with your kids" Jesus (available in a figurine), or the "Forgives me for spending the money I told my wife went in the tithe envelope but instead went to my girlfriend" Jesus. Upscale White Midwesterners have the "Jesus who mows our yard" but that's actually another Jesus entirely.

19. BEING MONOLINGUAL

Aside from the French we might have taken in the tenth grade (*Merci pour le pamplemousse, mademoiselle*), White Midwesterners are monolingual and we're proud of it, thank you very much. White Midwesterners are *so* not bilingual that we will absolutely massacre a foreign word, just to be obstinate about it. There are more than a few White Midwesterners who refer to tortillas as, "Tor-TILL-ee-yahs" and order "Eye-talian" dressing. And for the love of Job, do *not* take a White Midwesterner to a sushi restaurant—EVER.

20. HOMESCHOOLING

Oh, you've seen them—weirdo kids with their weirdo-moms. And by weird I mean they can watch *Napoleon Dynamite* and not get how weird Napoleon's family is. (Mom is usually wearing a jumper and knee socks and the kids are wearing dress clothes or some other ridiculous get-up.) Often the kids are holding some kind of sign, like "I'm happy my mom didn't abort me" or "Evolution is a myth" or some such nonsense. And when they leave the rally in the Suburban Assault Vehicle with the anti-Darwinism bumper stickers, they'll run you over getting out of the parking lot.

21. HATING EVOLUTION

You can't get much more White Midwestern than Kansas, so it should be no surprise that Kansas has been on the forefront of making sure children know that believing in the theory of evolution is optional. Apparently to these people believing the theory of gravity is optional too. Next thing you know your kids' physics book will have a sticker on it that says, "This textbook contains material on gravity. Gravity is a theory, not a fact, regarding how stuff stays on the ground and doesn't just come flying up at you. This material should be approached with an open mind, studied carefully, and critically considered."

22. SHOTGUN WEDDINGS

Recently, Kansas state senators approved a bill that prohibits anybody under age fifteen from getting married. This all started because some twenty-two-year-old from Falls City, Nebraska, got a fourteen-year-old girl pregnant. (They started dating when she was thirteen and he was twenty-one. So you know, it's not creepy or nothin'...) Anywho, like white-trash girls everywhere, she done turned up pregnant. The girl's mom said the two could get married, but you have to be at least seventeen to get married in Nebraska. Kansas didn't have a minimum age if there was parental approval, so the Falls City hillbillies loaded up the truck and they went to Hiawatha. Kansas, that is. Swimmin' pools ... Casey's Stores. (Sorry, I was on a roll.) There was actually a Kansas state senator who voted against this bill because of—wait for it—"Pro-Life considerations."

23. BEING THE ONLY PEOPLE ON EARTH WHO KNOW HOW TO COOK A STEAK

One thing unifies the Midwest unlike any other—the fact that we are the only people on Earth who know how to cook a steak. It's no coincidence that Charlie Trotter's famous steakhouse is located in Chicago or that Omaha Steaks is located in, well, Omaha. Yeah, yeah, we hear "y'all" Texans whining about how we don't cook it right, but you're wrong. Midwestern beef is the best stuff this side of Kobe, Japan. Frankly, there's a healthy segment of us who get downright perturbed when we open a menu and some East Coaster has called a perfectly good KC Strip a—*gasp*—New York Strip. Just how many beef cattle do you people think are raised in New York? If their beef tastes like their water, thanks, but I'll pass.

24. MALL BANGS

Back when we all still thought George Michael was straight, mall bangs were The Big Thing. No girl—of any ethnicity or geographic origin—would be caught dead outside her house unless those bangs were standin' up nice and proud. For many of us, we left those back when the Clintons got a hold of the White House but not every gal in the Midwest got the news, because I guarantee you that if you go into a Midwestern mall you will find some woman proudly sporting mall bangs. (Bonus points if she's wearing a scrunchie.) You see, White Midwesterners generally think that spending more than about twenty-five dollars for a woman's haircut is just idiotic, hence the bountiful abundance of Fantastic Sam's, Great Clips, and small-town beauty shops. If the best beauty operator in your town is named Pearl, Connie, or Flo, then you probably have mall bangs—whether you want them or not.

25. BEIGE

If there is one color that just screams, “Hey—I’m a practical White Midwesterner with a secure job in middle management,” it’s beige. Beige goes with *everything*. Oh, sure, black is sophisticated, but it’s just too impractical for White Midwesterners—it fades after a few washings. It’s just too dreary. And you can’t paint your house black—the neighbors will think you’re Satanists. Empirical evidence (that I just made up) proves that the happiness of a WM family is directly proportional to the amount of beige in its vicinity. That’s why affluent White Midwesterners live in beige-only subdivisions, drive beige Volvos, have dishwater-blonde beige hair, and wear beige slacks from Banana Republic. You just can’t go wrong with it.

26. WHITE ZINFANDEL

You know that memo that went out around 1992 about White Zinfandel wine no longer being cool? Yeah—'pparently didn't make it to the Midwest. White Midwesterners proudly order it from the drink menu at Ruby Tuesday as if they were ordering an entire bottle of Château Lafite-Rothschild. Smugly, a WM woman will announce to no one in particular, "Well, *I'm* going to have the White Zinfandel," as if she's announcing to no one in particular that she just took up contract-killing or bisexuality. Ears perk up at nearby tables, "She's having the Zinfandel? Next thing you know she'll be hosting swingers' parties. Better tell Trevor he can't mow her lawn anymore. There's no telling what that woman will do next."

27. SMALL-MARKET BASEBALL TEAMS

Oh, you fancy-pants people on the coasts can have your Yankees and Dodgers—White Midwesterners are happy with our Royals, Twins, Brewers, Cardinals, Reds, and Pirates. Well, I shouldn't say "happy," because Royals fans haven't been happy since they beat St. Louis in the I-70 World Series back in 1985. But we still take the family to the ballpark on Buck Night (which will actually set you back about forty dollars) and White Midwesterners will stand in line for two hours in the freezing cold for a free Billy Butler jersey. Because one of these years, I promise you . . .

2

28. DRESSING DOWN WHEN TRAVELING

If you spend any time at an airport, you can play a quick game of "pick out the White Midwesterner." White Midwesterners, for one, do not dress up to travel. *Ever*. WMs see absolutely no need in impressing anyone on a plane. Spend some time in a Midwestern airport and the majority of the travelers—especially on weekends—are wearing clothes that people from elsewhere wouldn't be caught dead wearing. A KU sweatshirt from 1992? No sweat. Dress pants (pleated, thankyouverymuch) with a hole in the back pocket? Sure thing. Ball cap with (insert name of state university) logo? Wouldn't leave the house without it. Why wear tennis shoes with laces when Velcro shoes are easy on, easy off? Why wear skin-tight jeans when jogging pants are comfortable and won't set off the metal detectors? "It ain't a fashion show, Connie; it's Southwest."

29. BILL O'REILLY

Well, *somebody* has to be watching his show, and it sure as heck isn't all those Godless communists who live on the East Coast or the "fruits, nuts, and flakes" who live in California. Bill O'Reilly is really the only New Yorker whom White Midwesterners trust—he's looking out for *us*.

30. TRACK SUITS

Fat people (i.e., White Midwesterners) love track suits. They're kicky, stretchy, and often water-repellent—what's not to love? Plus it's one of the few times when Carl from down the cul-de-sac puts on a color other than beige.

31. CHILD ONE-UPMANSHIP CAR ART

Back in my day (you know, the '80s), all the latchkey kids were admonished to not wear their names on anything lest they get picked up by some child molester or Jehovah's Witness or some other such horror. I don't know when it started, but sometime after my parents' brilliant children got out of school the trend of emblazoning your child's name, sport of choice, and jersey number on the family AstroVan took hold. Especially in White Midwestern suburbs you can't cut somebody off in traffic without being greeted with "Brianna ⚽ #22" on their van, as if you care what their Precious Snowflake does for recreation. (For Mother's Day I offered to sticker my parents' new Lincoln Town Car with "Cara, Jack Daniel's, #69." They declined.)

SMN INDIANS
BAND
KENNA

32. RVS

I never noticed how much White Midwesterners like RVs—then my White Midwestern parents retired. My mom likes their RV because, "Well, when you stay in hotels you have to deal with *other* people's dirt, but with our RV we just have *our* dirt." And my dad likes it because it gives him an excuse to trade in the well-worn family sedan for the biggest dang pickup you've seen not pulling a horse trailer. RV parks are chock full of White Midwesterners, and easy conversations start with, "Say, how d'ya like that Eye-Tasca ya got there? Oh, we've had this Prairie Schooner for a few years now—the wife threw *a fit* when I got it butcha can't get her out of it now, I tell ya. Say, what's your name again?"

33. FLORIDA

You know it's not just the Seinfelds and the Costanzas who dreamed of retiring in Del Boca Vista—there are plenty of White Midwesterners who retire there, too. It's like there's some unwritten White Midwestern Rule that retirement = snowbirding in Florida, usually on "the gulf side." Unlike the richer East-Coast types, White Midwesterners will move down and live half the year in trailers. (Yes, the same people who live in Tornado Alley see no problem in dropping a chunk of retirement change into a snazzy doublewide in a nice trailer park in Hurricane-Magnet, Florida.) The same kinds of trailers they wouldn't be caught dead in up in the Midwest are flat-out status symbols in Florida. The best are "park models" with "Florida Rooms" built into the sides of them, and no retiree is fully set without a three-wheeled bicycle.

13
13
13
Garden MORE work less

34. THE AUTO INDUSTRY

Other than agriculture, one of the biggest industries in the Midwest is the auto industry. Michigan alone has about a third of the U.S. auto industry jobs. Midwesterners love the auto industry because it's one of the few places where you can make a nice living without a college degree—and by nice I mean "makes more than a lot of people who have MBAs" nice.

35. ACRYLIC NAILS WITH FRENCH MANICURES

Guilty as charged: We White Midwesterners *love* French manicures, and we don't give a hoot if some size zero fashionista in New York thinks it's déclassé. No bride would be caught on her wedding day without it and no White Midwestern soccer mom would be caught at little Trevor's game without her acrylic French manicure. We don't care if you think it's tacky—we love them. Even if it takes an act of God to help us open a soda can.

36. FIGHTING OVER WHETHER IT'S POP OR SODA

White Midwesterners tend to be fairly agreeable types, but one thing that we will never agree on is whether that fizzy carbonated beverage you have right there should be called soda or pop. Now, it's not just "soda" or "pop," but depending on where you are in the Midwest your choices are actually "soohhh-duh" or "paaaaaahhhp" or "coke." Honestly—more late-night dorm room fights have begun over the soda versus pop controversy than whether the nerdy guy in the room across the hall is getting it on with your girlfriend. (He is. And so is your roommate.)

37. COLLEGE RIVALRIES

You big-city types can get your panties all in a bunch fighting over the Red Sox versus Yankees or Letterman versus Leno or the Yale versus MIT rowing clubs or whatever it is you people on the East Coast are into. In the Midwest it's all about college sports rivalries. My mother (an Iowa State graduate) told me that she'd pay for me to go to college anywhere except for the University of Nebraska because of how obnoxious their fans are. And if you're talking about two teams from the same state—KU versus K-State, Iowa State versus Iowa—well, put on your pads because things are gonna get ugly.

TIKI B

38. THEME BARS

Did you know that in some parts of the world there is just a place called a "bar"? They no longer exist in the Midwest. Now all bars have to be characterized as Sports Bars or Karaoke Bars or Juice Bars or whatever else some marketing executive in Chicago can come up with. Even dirty old pool halls are now sickeningly family-friendly ("It's no smoking in here, sir—little Carson is trying to eat his chicken strips").

39. FINISHED BASEMENTS

One of the first things that shocks—*shocks!*—White Midwestern expatriates is the fact that in many parts of the country houses don't come with basements. To us, that's like houses not having faucets. White Midwesterners not only have basements, we trick them out with pool tables and wetbars. When you tell a WM that you don't have a basement, the first thing that pops into our minds is, "Where do you go when the tornado sirens go off?" Seriously—not having a basement is just beyond us.

40. WOOD PANELING

Speaking of finished basements, White Midwesterners have a fetish for wood paneling. Need to wall off a room into two spaces? Wood paneling. Want to turn your garage into a rumpus room? Wood paneling. White Midwesterners think wood paneling cures just about every architectural ill for an affordable price. What's not to love? Well, other than the fact that (a) it's rarely wood, (b) it smells horrific, and (c) it sucks all light out of the room more efficiently than the densest black hole, it's a snazzy home improvement tool. If you've moved to the Midwest from the coast and are feeling depressed, it's not Seasonal Affective Disorder; it's likely the fact that you have wood paneling.

41. WHITE CASTLE

If you love weirdly steamed mini-burgers after a night of drinking and/or pot smoking, you have one place to thank—Wichita, Kansas. Yes, White Castle was founded in the good old Midwest long before McDonald's (also a White Midwestern creation). Even though it's firmly a White Midwestern food (duh, it's first word is "white") it has been immortalized in pop culture, from *Harold and Kumar Go to White Castle* (I and II) to no fewer than five Beastie Boys songs.

42. MLMS

I don't know if we're gullible or just entrepreneurial in spirit, but damned near every White Midwestern woman has been an "independent consultant" for some kind of multi-level marketing (MLM) company. The merchandise is sold at a "party," usually held in the home of the White Midwestern consultant's sister-in-law. Guests ooh and ahh at overpriced gee-gaws such as pizza stones or three-wick candles or tacky lingerie while noshing on chips and salsa, Alco-pop, and a cream cheese and fruit pizza.

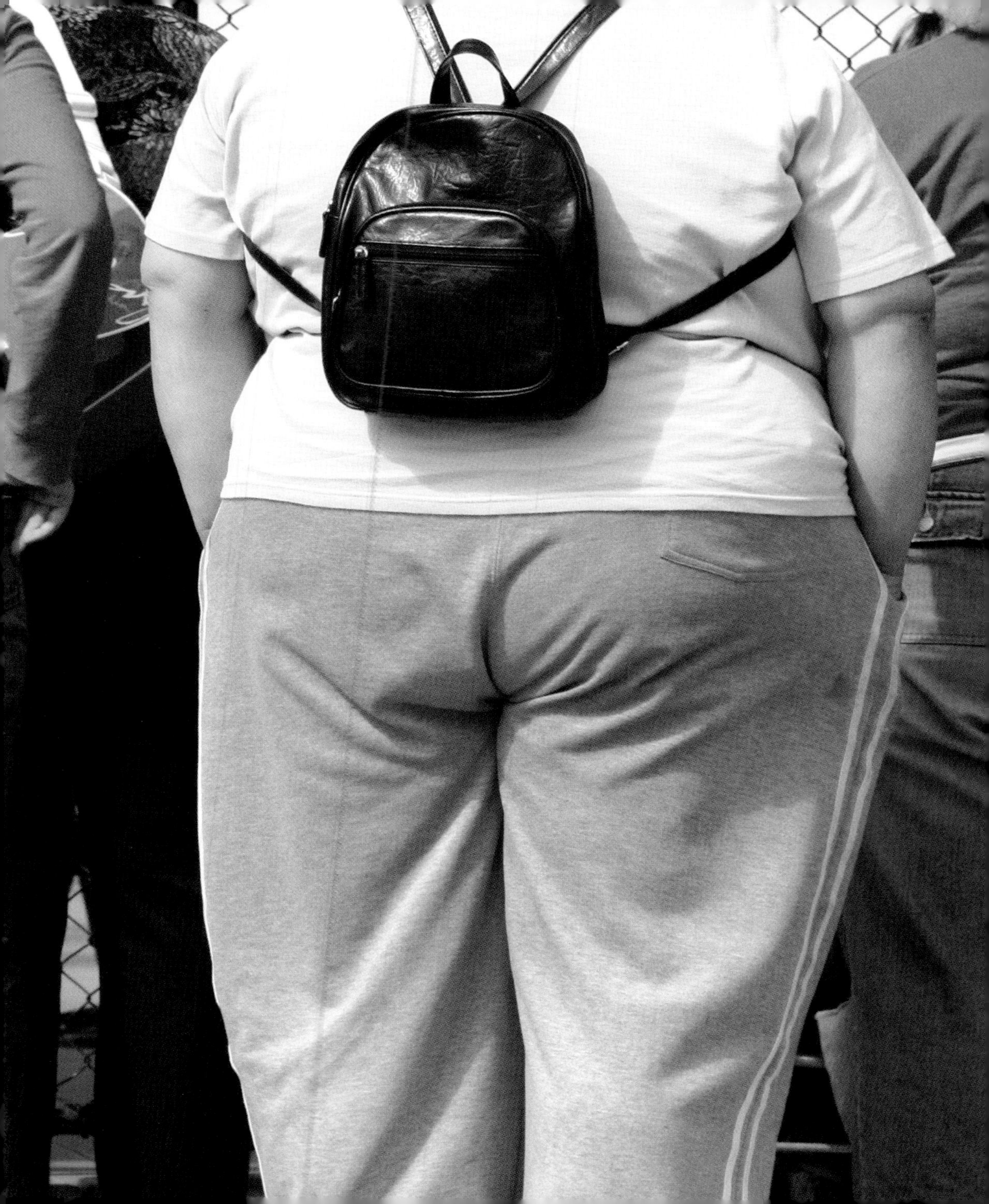

43. DRESSY SWEATS

We've already discussed the track suit as high White Midwestern fashion, but the trend doesn't just stop there—White Midwesterners make a distinction between their "regular" (hole-laden) sweats that they wear to mow the lawn and "dressy sweats" that you can wear to a graduation or funeral or court date. (I am not kidding—hang out in a courtroom for a day in a small Midwestern county.) Dressy sweats for women include some kind of yoga-type pants and a hot pink hoodie, whereas dressy sweats for men are typically black and contain some element stripe down the leg and an Under Armor shirt. Dressy sweats say, "I'm just as chic as those women on *The Real Housewives of Orange County* but I'm still keepin' it real in my elastic waistband pants."

44. FAKE MARTINIS

What goes in a martini? Well, if you ask a White Midwesterner, a martini is whatever you put into a martini glass. (There's a wicked martini in Kansas City that is rimmed with—wait for it—*Tang.*) You can have Kool-Aid martinis as far as WMs are concerned, and we don't care what you so-called purists think of it. You're probably the same suckers who pay more than fifteen dollars for a bottle of wine.

45. PLEATHER

This is a fashion trend that *Just*. *Needs. To. Stop*. For the love of Cher, people—the Midwest is full of cattle, yet for some godforsaken reason White Midwesterners have started to incorporate pleather into our wardrobes. (Personally, I blame PETA.)

46. PUTTING "R"S WHERE THEY DON'T BELONG

You know how people in Boston conveniently leave out "r"s that belong in the pronunciation of a word? Well, all those "r"s traveled west and landed in the Midwest. My dad—God bless him—is the absolute worst offender at putting "r"s where they don't belong. Where did he go on his class trip? WARSHington, D.C. (My western Iowan mom's not much better—her "r"s are softer so it sounds like she's doing the "woish.") St. Louisans go so far as to make a hard-r part of the word: Clergy there refer to "R holy Lard and Gahd."

47. HOME SHOPPING

You always wondered, "Who in the hell buys all that Quacker Factory junk on QVC?" but I'm here to tell you—it's Connie in Davenport, Iowa, and Mindy in Bloomington, Indiana, and about 12 million other White Midwestern women. Remember, White Midwesterners are exceedingly practical people, so if that nice Jeanne Bice gal is going to keep making clothes that we can order right off the TV without trying to corral Carl and the kids into the AstroVan, then we're just gonna keep buying them. Besides, you can't get that Floral Garden Mandarin Collar Stretch Jacket with Removable Rhinestones *just anywhere*, you know?

48. ABOVE-GROUND POOLS

The weather in any given Midwestern town ranges from subzero to scorching hot, sometimes within the same week. No matter, that above ground swimming pool can do double-duty as an ice-skating pond and a place where you can teach your Precious Snowflakes how to do the breast stroke in the comfort of your own back yard. Above-ground pools, though they look tacky, are actually exceedingly more practical than the in-ground pools found in other parts of the country, which can't withstand the constant freezing and thawing that you get in the Midwest. (Feel free to share this knowledge with your seatmate the next time you are on a plane, as every good Midwesterner would.)

PELIGRO

49. ILLEGAL FIREWORKS

If you didn't know any better, you'd think the only reason that Missouri exists is to provide people from neighboring states the opportunity to buy fireworks. *Year round*. Thanks to a wacky wrinkle in the law, Missouri residents can only buy fireworks from June 20 through July 10 and from December 20th through January 2, but out-of-state residents can buy them year round. Personally I never realized the market for fireworks in, say, April . . .

50. INDOOR WATERPARKS

Back in the olden days (the ’70s), kids would grab a garden hose and a cheap metal sprinkler and voilà—hours of summertime fun. Then came outdoor waterparks and now, so as not to subject our White selves to the browning rays of the sun, comes the indoor waterpark. Whether it’s a Great Wolf Lodge or Schlitterbahn, the indoor waterpark is the best investment since Microsoft was just some little company with a geeky owner.

51. STATE FAIRS/ COUNTY FAIRS

What's less pleasant than humid August heat? Humid August heat plus the fragrant odors of livestock. Leave it to White Midwesterners to create a family destination for this fun-filled experience. Unless your family farms there is no reason on God's green Earth to prance around in stinky show barns and get sawdust and chigger bites all over. Well, there is *one* reason—funnel cakes—but that's the *only* reason.

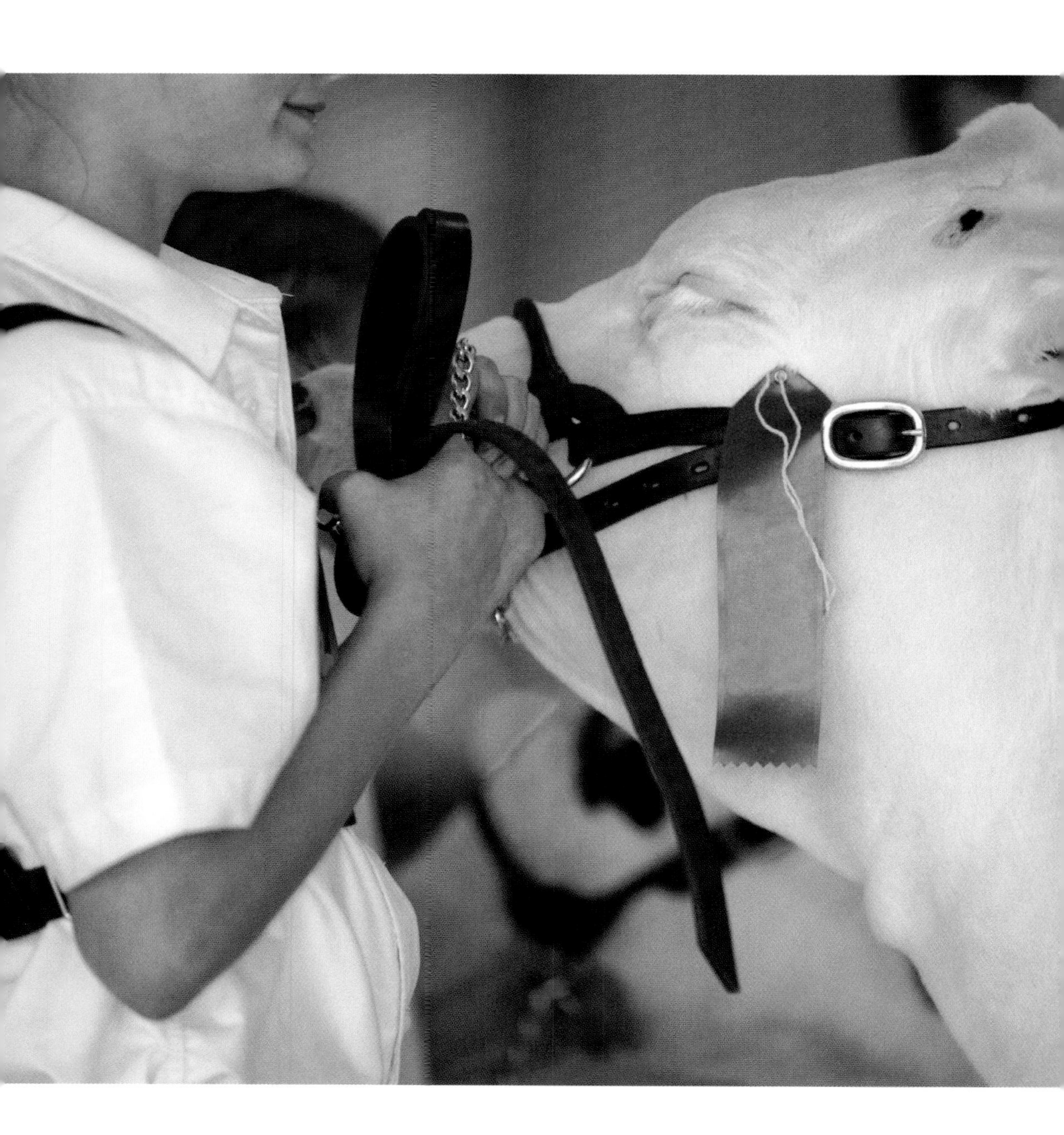

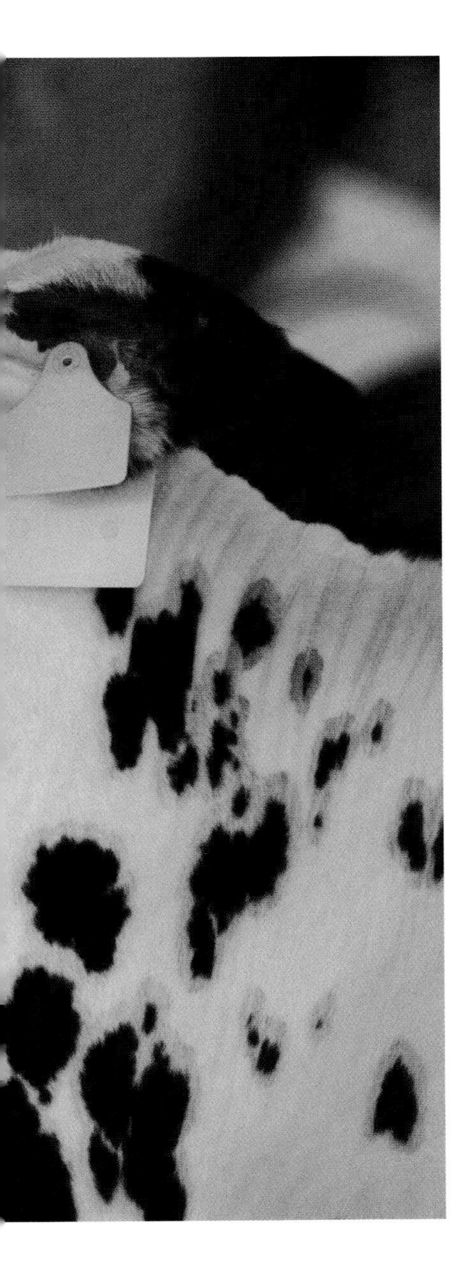

52. 4-H

Being in 4-H is still a *very* big deal to White Midwesterners. Even when farm families move to "town," they (misguidedly) put their kids in 4-H so that they don't lose a sense of their history. (Besides, who else is going to teach your kid to spin wool?) I know—my Iowa-born parents enrolled my brother and me in our local 4-H club. (I won a State Fair ribbon for my snickerdoodle cookies—at my school you couldn't get less cool than this unless you, well, spun your own wool.)

53. THE WEATHER CHANNEL

There's a saying in the Midwest that if you don't like the weather, wait a few minutes. Temperatures in the Midwest range from "so flipping cold" to "so flipping hot," sometimes within the same flipping day. People in other parts of the country turn on the Weather Channel to see if they should bring a light jacket with them to the trendy espresso bar; White Midwesterners check the Weather Channel to see if we should bring subzero de-icer, sunscreen, and an umbrella to go get the mail.

54. CASEY'S GENERAL STORES

If your Midwestern town doesn't have a Casey's General Store, your town is strictly jerkwater—end of story. There are over 1,400 Casey's stores in the Midwest, most of them in small towns. Next time you're cruising along a state highway and you're in need of a donut, a beer, and some ammo for your 12-gauge shotgun, just pull into the local Casey's.

CASEY'S
GENERAL STORE
HOMEMADE
PIZZA
To Go
CASEY'S
General
Store

55. FOOD

Just take a look at your average WM and you'll notice that we don't push back from the dinner table any too soon, if you catch my drift. WMs love food, whether it's Kansas City barbecue, Wisconsin cheese and brats, Chicago-style pizza, or the Twin Cities' very own corn dog. We chomp it down like there's no tomorrow. If you're ever in Iowa or Wisconsin, do yourself a big favor and find a Maid-Rite restaurant—you won't be sorry.

56. GOATEES

Know an easy way to pick the White Midwestern guy out of a lineup? He's the dude with the goatee. Yes, the facial hair fashion that wore out its welcome around 1996 everywhere else in the world is still a viable option in the Midwest. Goatees are an emblem of Midwestern practicality: Why shave your whole face when you can just shave from your earlobes to your jaw line? Think of the time you'll save!

57. TALKING ABOUT THE WEATHER

The easiest way to start a conversation with a White Midwesterner is to bring up the weather. This is because *our weather sucks*. And even though everyone who has lived in the Midwest for more than, oh, eight minutes knows that *our weather sucks*, we are still baffled at how terrible our weather is. Seriously, you can sit down next to a stranger and simply utter the words, “This weather ...” and voilà—instant rapport.

58. *CONSUMER REPORTS*

There is one publication that is almost as sacred as the Bible to White Midwesterners: *Consumer Reports*. White Midwesterners love handy reference materials and *Consumer Reports* is the Farmer's Almanac of the Information Age. I actually know White Midwesterners who will not throw out old *Consumer Reports* in the event they want to purchase a used item out of the classifieds and don't want to get ripped off. (Seriously, if you are in the market for a 1990s-era vacuum, I know a guy who can steer you in the right direction.)

59. TORNADOES

Honestly, as I write this there are tornado sirens going off all over the Midwest. Now a normal, rational human being hearing a tornado siren will run inside to the lowest part of their domicile, assume the crash position, and hang on until either the all-clear siren sounds or you can see daylight through your basement ceiling. *Not real Midwesterners*. Real White Midwesterners run outside and try to figure where the tornado is and how long it will take to get to wherever they are. If a siren goes off in your part of town and you don't see your neighbors out on their driveways, it's probably because they're still trying to find their video cameras. There are people who have forgotten to videotape every one of their children's birthdays but have hours upon hours of "almost a tornado" footage. By the way, no real Midwesterner will *ever* refer to a tornado as a "twister"—only idiotic TV personalities do. Tell your friends.

60. PICKUP TRUCKS

When people think of pickups they tend to think of the South, but there's a big difference between a Midwesterner's pickup and a Southerner's. Southerners have pickups because they need just one more place to sport a Confederate Flag and hang a gun rack, while Midwesterners actually use their pickups to *do things*, like haul that year's worth of toilet paper we bought at Sam's Club.

61. AFFORDABLE HOUSES

You can buy an enormous house in the Midwest for seven dollars. OK, maybe not that low, but compared to the coasts you can get a great big house in, say, Milwaukee for what a 400 square foot condo would cost in Modesto, California. We know this because we like to look at the real estate listings in your newspapers when we visit. And laugh. In fact, that's one of the things that former Midwesterners miss the most about living here. That and the relative lack of California nutjobs.

62. KNOWING ABOUT FARMING (OR AT LEAST KNOWING MORE THAN YOU)

People who aren't from here seem to think that everyone in the Midwest was born on a farm. While agriculture is still a big part of the Midwestern economy, there's a whole slew of us White Midwesterners who haven't stepped foot on a farm since our fifth-grade field trip. Regardless, we still know a thing or two about farming: Corn is supposed to be knee high by the Fourth of July, soybeans are a nitrogen-fixing plant, and you can make a bunch of meth if you get your hands on some anhydrous ammonia. Farming *rules.*

63. WAL-MART

You know all those people who whine and moan about how Wal-Mart is killing the small mom-and-pop stores in the Midwest? Yeah, they are all from not-the-Midwest. Real White Midwesterners will put on their calendars when the next Wal-Mart is due to appear in their counties. That's because you can do everything at Wal-Mart—tune up your hearing aid, get your nails done, open a new checking account, cut your hair, and pick up some shotgun shells and baby shoes on your way to getting your tires rotated. This is why White Midwesterners are so fat: When you have everything in one place, who needs to walk anywhere?

MART®
$9.96

Cracker Barrel
Old Country Store

64. CRACKER BARREL

Have you ever been in a Cracker Barrel? If one of your White Midwestern gift-giving relatives has, you are likely the proud(?) recipient of "the cutest darned quilted patriotic kitty-cat sweatshirt with matching socks I've ever seen!" After all, you didn't really want an iPod for your birthday now, did ya?

65. SUN TEA

Quick—if you look at my neighbor's patio you will see not one but *two* jars of sun tea. White Midwesterners will go mad for the stuff. Personally, I don't get the whole sun tea phenomenon—why take five hours to heat up water when you can do it on the stove in five minutes? Midwestern sun tea drinkers will swear on a stack of Protestant Bibles that tea made with water that's been sitting out in the sun all day tastes better than boiled water and is—get this—more energy efficient. Of course, when they stop driving their 12-MPG pickups to the store to get the stinkin' tea, I might start believing them.

66. TOKEN ETHNIC FRIENDS

Most White Midwesterners have a token "ethnic" friend. We have them because we don't want people to think we're not "with it." If you are an affluent White Midwesterner your token ethnic friend is probably Indian (not the kinds with the casinos—the other kind) or maybe Korean, which is fine—your kid can cheat off of their kid in math class.

67. GOOD STATE COLLEGES

East Coasters have the Ivy League and California has Stanford, but if you really want a quality education, you need look no further than your average Midwestern state college. The prices are more affordable, the towns are usually small, and weed is incredibly cheap, what with all the surrounding farmland on which to grow it.

68. BRANSON, MISSOURI

Sophisticated people have Broadway; White Midwesterners have Branson. Yes, the place where entertainers you thought were dead years ago still pack in the blue-haired crowds. (Yakov Smirnoff, anyone?) Travelers to Branson are greeted with horrendous traffic and the finest collection of tacky billboards this side of Reno. If country music doesn't strike your fancy, there's always the fish hatchery or the Shepherd of the Hills. Or a self-inflicted gunshot wound to the spleen.

ANTIQUES

69. ANTIQUE MALLS

The Midwest is more boring than, say, macrame, so a lot of White Midwesterners collect old stuff as a hobby. Junk shops have grown up and are now these behemoth, side-of-the-road antique malls. Most Midwestern antique malls have crazy names like "The Brass Armadillo" or "Clyde 'n Clara's Clutter Cabin" and have about fifty years' worth of junk that used to be in your grandma's house (and smells like it, too). Who knew there'd be such a market for Listerine-scented doilies?

70. THEME PARKS

White Midwestern theme parks come in about five flavors, all of which involve kitschy-themed rides, eight-dollar hamburgers, and lots—and I mean *lots*—of horrible theme park art, conveniently available for purchase in the gift shops located throughout the park. It must be the heady odors of the asphalt sidewalks, but somehow every trip to a Midwestern theme park involves the purchase of some blown-glass figurine that won't even make it to the car in one piece. If you look closely, just about every White Midwestern home has a blown-glass swan with a glued-together neck displayed in the back of the curio cabinet, referred to as "The Swan from the Day Danny Made Mom Cry."

71. OLD-TIMEY PHOTOS

No visit to a White Midwestern theme park would be complete without the family old-timey photo. White Midwesterners love old-timey photos because it gives us a chance to look exotic while still looking White. And Midwestern. Yes, you too can dress up like Colonel Caleb McHenry, that old Civil War hero you always wanted to be, instead of Kevin McHenry who works in tech support at State Farm Insurance and has an ex-wife and two kids who have spent too much time sitting in front of the microwave, if you catch my drift.

REWARD
REWARD!
WELLS FARGO & CO'S
WELLS

72. SUNFLOWERS

You can instantly tell if someone is a transplant to the Midwest because they don't seem to have sunflower-motif items *anywhere* in their house. This, friends, is sacrilege. First of all, sunflowers are cheery and bright, and secondly, they just look darling next to white wicker furniture.

73. FREE REFILLS

Nothing frosts a White Midwesterner's donuts faster than a restaurant that doesn't offer free refills. This is such an affront that it can mar an otherwise perfectly lovely vacation. "Well, yes, dear, your Aunt Marlo and I did enjoy ourselves in Paris—but it was almost ruined by the fact that they don't offer free refills there! Can you imagine? No wonder they lost their empire; they're just not a charitable people."

74. NIKES

Oh sure, you see those uppity folks from *other* parts of the country wearing Merrells or Adidas or New Balance, but here in the Midwest we like our Nikes. We like that comforting swoosh and "Just Do It" motto, which nicely sums up the Midwestern work ethic. Nikes are familiar to us—they've been around for years and they certainly didn't hurt Michael Jordan any, so why change brands if we don't have to? Oh sure, there was that whole sweatshop controversy, but that all blew over.

75. CHRISTMAS LETTERS

If you ever want to see a time capsule of a WM family's life, you need not look any further than the yearly Christmas letter. They all seem to follow the same rubric: apology for not keeping in touch as often as they should, followed by a recap of the family's year including children's accomplishments, vacations taken, and hospital visits (selves and relatives within the first degree), and closing with either something funny about the family pet or a reminder about how Jesus is the "Reason for the Season." Optional paragraphs include a recap of the year's weather (farm families) or a bizarre political rant (this is the part of the Christmas letter that the wife lets her husband write).

76. FAKE FLOWERS

Remember, White Midwesterners are nothing if not practical, though sometimes our practicality transverses the sublime to the ridiculous. Here is Nellie Hopkey from East Moline, Illinois, to explain: "Gosh, ya know—real flowers are just so g-d expensive, why not just get some real-looking flowers that don't attract fruit flies and die in a week? And I'd hate to cut some from Carl's rosebushes—he just agonizes over those things. Besides, these royal blue roses with the faux water droplets on them are just so much prettier than the real thing." That explains it all.

77. WEDDING RECEPTIONS AT THE VFW

If you've lived in the Midwest for any length of time you've probably attended a wedding, and the reception for said wedding was likely held in the town's VFW hall. Of course, decorating the VFW takes some creativity (see Fake Flowers, number 76) but with the right lighting and some cinnamon-scented Glade you can really turn these patriotic gin joints into something to behold. Plus, VFW receptions are usually catered by the local grocery store, so your guests will likely be too busy digging into their Hy-Vee fried chicken and mashed potatoes to even notice that gigantic Pabst Blue Ribbon sign above the bride's head.

78. TIMESHARES

For the promise of a free digital camera, White Midwesterners will empty little Brittany's college savings account to "invest" in a $10,000 timeshare. Face it—White Midwesterners crave familiarity. So when it comes to family travel, why go to a different place every year when you can spend every summer vacation at the Lake of the Ozarks? Besides, who wants to undergo the torment of choosing a vacation spot and the sheer agony of booking travel—using the computer?!—when you can sit back and relax at your "little place on the lake"?

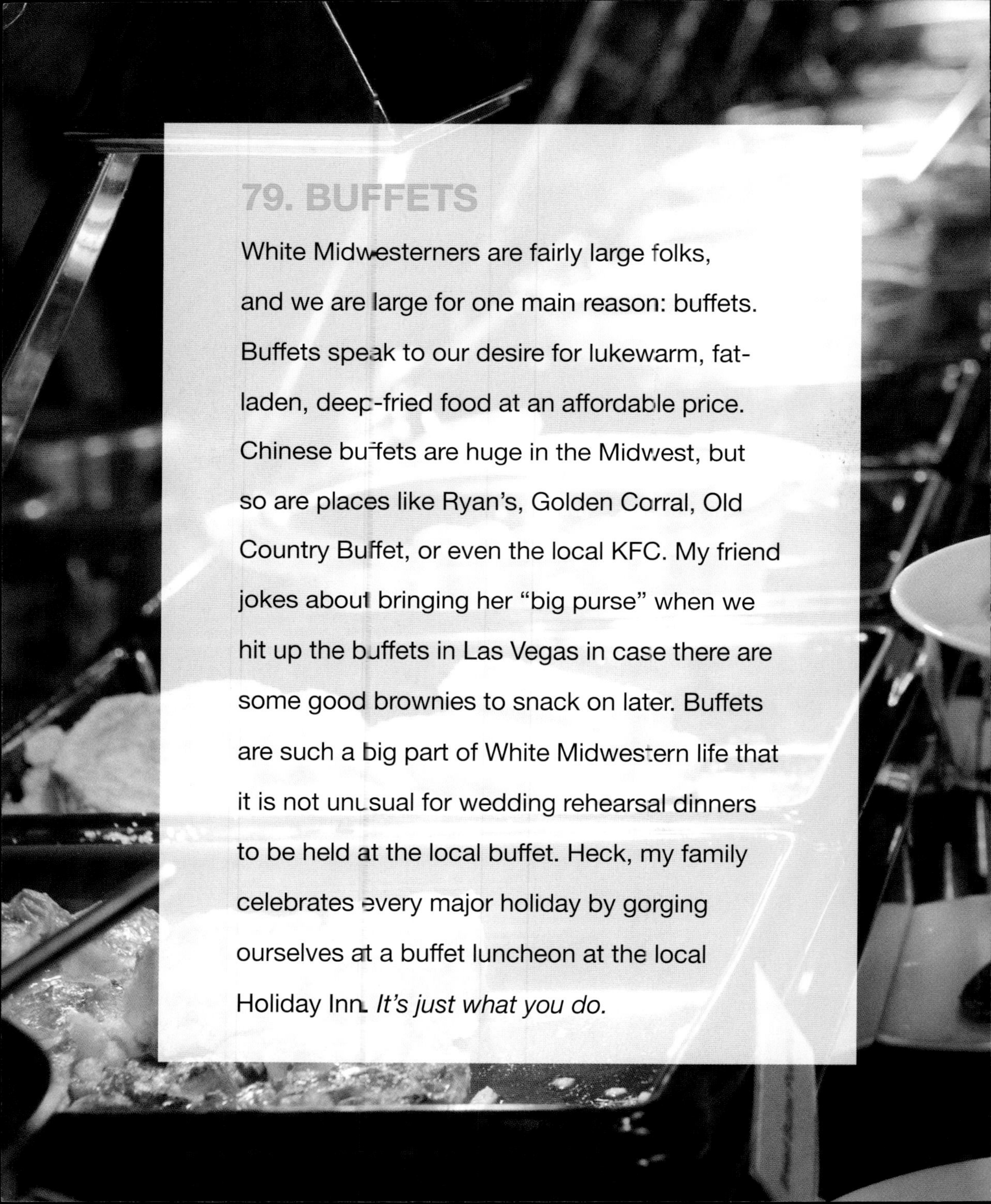

79. BUFFETS

White Midwesterners are fairly large folks, and we are large for one main reason: buffets. Buffets speak to our desire for lukewarm, fat-laden, deep-fried food at an affordable price. Chinese buffets are huge in the Midwest, but so are places like Ryan's, Golden Corral, Old Country Buffet, or even the local KFC. My friend jokes about bringing her "big purse" when we hit up the buffets in Las Vegas in case there are some good brownies to snack on later. Buffets are such a big part of White Midwestern life that it is not unusual for wedding rehearsal dinners to be held at the local buffet. Heck, my family celebrates every major holiday by gorging ourselves at a buffet luncheon at the local Holiday Inn. *It's just what you do.*

80. AWFUL NAMES FOR KIDS

While much of the WM lifestyle is fairly conservative, there is an insidious plague that is sweeping across the prairie, and that plague is known as the Carson-ization of America. Back in the day, boys had boy names and girls were named either (a) Jennifer or (b) Stephanie, and everything was right with the world. Then somehow White Midwesterners decided to start giving their kids names that actually make them seem even more White but that are actually really, really ridiculous. There's some poor child in Milwaukee who is probably named "Smith Huffnagel" or a kid in Stanley, Wisconsin, named "Riley Bjorklund."

81. SCHWAN'S FROZEN FOODS

If you haven't seen a beigey-yellow Schwan's Food delivery van in your neighborhood, *you are missing out*. Women in the Midwest go absolutely crackers when the "Schwan's Man" comes, delivering enough ice cream and frozen dinners to feed a family of twelve. (Part of me thinks that two or three of those kids actually belong to the Schwan's man, but I don't pry.) Schwan's is a boon to farm families and people who live out in the boonies: They can place their order a week in advance (or now on the Internet) and they don't have to drive "to town" to get lots of high-quality food. How practical is that?

82. PANTYHOSE

Fashionistas on the coasts will tell you that wearing pantyhose is a fashion crime, but not to White Midwesterners. We're so addicted to pantyhose that some (older) White Midwestern women insist on wearing them with capris and sandals—hence sandal-foot style hosiery. It's just unseemly for women in the Midwest to dress up without them. Plus, just because your pantyhose has a run in it doesn't mean it's useless—why, you can use it to tie up your tomato plants, make a handy loofah, or tie down the trunk of your car!

83. CRAB RANGOON

If you live in the Midwest you know what crab rangoons are, but I was shocked—*shocked*—when I went to San Francisco and no one had a clue what I was talking about. "You know, those pyramid-ish shaped things with cream cheese and crab in them? That you fry?" I said to the nice lady at the Chinese restaurant. She shook her head slowly. "They're *Chinese*," I repeated, as if to jog her memory. (Never mind that Rangoon is actually in Burma—to us everything "oriental" is Chinese just the same as anybody speaking Spanish is Mexican.) Still no clue. But White Midwesterners know what they are, and they know that you get two of them with a combo plate. Too bad those poor people in San Francisco are missing out.

84. STOICISM

To many people the word "stoic" always precedes the word "Midwesterner." While Brits have perfected the stiff upper lip, it is true that White Midwesterners run a close second when it comes to not being terribly emotionally demonstrative. That's why White Midwesterners like Tom Brokaw (from North Dakota) and Walter Cronkite (from Missouri) made the best television news anchors—we're fairly unflappable. To us, emotional outbursts are a sign of poor self-control, so outside of sports they make us terribly uncomfortable.

NO
PARKING
SPEED
LIMIT
25
WARNING
NEIGHBORHOOD WATC

85. PRECIOUS MOMENTS PARK AND CHAPEL

You know those creepy little figurines that well-meaning relatives give you instead of the Prince Greatest Hits album you wanted for your birthday? Well, the fine folks at Precious Moments have their very own Precious Moments Park and Chapel in Carthage, Missouri. And no, it's not just any chapel: "Inspired by Michelangelo's Sistine Chapel in Rome, Precious Moments artist and creator, Samuel J. Butcher, designed and constructed the Precious Moments Chapel as his way of sharing the joy of his faith with the world, and it has become his crowning work." (That's from their Web site, www.preciousmoments.com/content.cfm/chapel.) Only the Sistine Chapel is a masterpiece and the Precious Moments Chapel is . . . awful.

86. BLACK MUSIC

Oh sure, that nice forty-something man in the Volvo next to you seems to be pleasantly driving at a reasonable speed. He must be listening to Garrison Keillor or maybe some Peter, Paul, and Mary? *Hardly.* When no one else is watching, White Midwesterners crank up the Black music like they were born in a recording booth at Motown Records. White Midwestern women love Aretha, Etta James, and Diana Ross, and White Midwestern men love Snoop Dogg, Dr. Dre, and maybe a little Barry White.

87. POTTERY BARN

Oh my heck, do we love Pottery Barn in the Midwest. To us it just screams "Sophisticated home furnishings that are durable and all go great with beige." Plus Pottery Barn stores are usually only found in the larger Midwestern cities, so getting to shop there is a mini-vacation in its own right. New homeowners will proudly show off their Pottery Barn furnishings as if they were precious antiques—"Well, yes, it's like Aunt Florence's old farm table, but it's better—it's *new*."

POTTERY BARN
sale

88. HALLMARK COLLECTIBLE ORNAMENTS

Did you ever wonder who actually bought all those Hallmark Collectible Ornaments? It's White Midwesterners. Partly because Hallmark is a Midwestern company (nestled in the gooey center of Kansas City, Missouri) and partly because the ornaments are just so festive without being ostentatious, White Midwesterners think they are the bee's knees. They are usually unveiled sometime in July, so people can order in plenty of time for Christmas. ("Planning ahead" is a competitive sport in the Midwest, probably owing to our farming history.)

89. THEME BATHROOMS

Can anybody just have a bathroom? Oh, not the White Midwesterner. White Midwestern bathrooms *must* have a theme—as if you'd accidentally pee in the kitchen sink were it not for the bright yellow duckies to show you the way. White Midwestern bathroom themes often involve one of the following: shells, "country," or Mickey Mouse. And they always involve the "good" towels that no one is ever allowed to use under penalty of death.

90. WHITE SUBURBS

If you ever want to find the largest concentration of White Midwesterners in any given Midwestern city, you must look no farther than the outermost ring of the city limits. White Midwesterners just feel more comfortable living with other people who are exactly like them, and those people are located in the suburbs. White suburbs are not complete without bizarrely named subdivisions, such as “Corporate Woods Hills” or “Surly Elk Estates,” and they are often paired with the blandest sounding street names you can dream up without being high on Valium. Bonus points if the suburb is located in a completely flat area and the streets all have names that include “mont,” “view,” or “hill,” such as Montview Drive, Hillmont Court, Hillview Circle. (It’s no wonder the Dominoes guy takes an hour to find your house.)

91. CINNAMON-SCENTED HOMES

I don't know when exactly they met, but there must have been some committee that got together and decided that White Midwestern homes should have a particular smell, and that smell would be cinnamon. Year round. It's as if cinnamon has replaced the smell of Clorox and Pine-Sol as the universal smell of "clean." In any given White Midwestern home you will find cinnamon potpourri, cinnamon candles, and cinnamon Glade under the bathroom sink—to all be used at once.

92. FLORAL WALLPAPER

If you aren't fortunate to live in God's White Midwest, then you probably think our houses look like something the Amish would live in. Not true. White Midwestern houses are never complete without floral wallpaper somewhere in the home. (Bonus points if it's sunflower floral wallpaper.) White Midwesterners love floral wallpaper because it is "cheery" and reminds them that the snow will eventually melt and—God willing—spring will eventually return.

93. ASIAN MASSAGE PARLORS

OK, this is an easy one—who *doesn't* like Asian massage parlors? OK, some wives, for one, and the women who have to work there. But obviously somebody likes them because just about every White Midwestern town has one or two "Suki Spas" or "Tokyo Saunas," usually located in the sketchy part of town that has the best highway access.

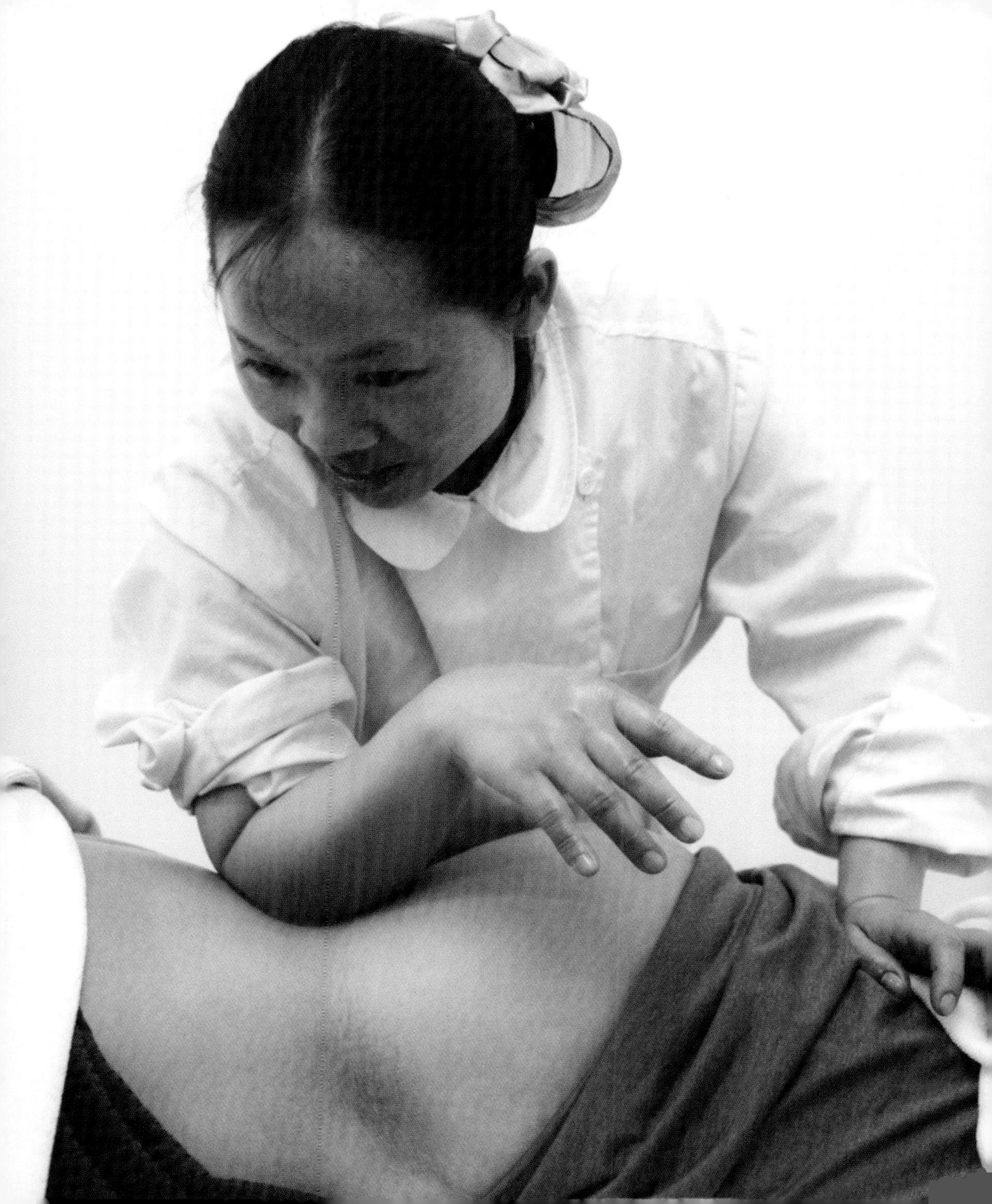

94. CRIPES

Yeah, I said it—*cripes.* And to that I'm adding *g-d* and *hades*, as in, "Cripes, Don, it's hotter than g-d hades in here—when are ya gonna fix the AC, huh?" White Midwesterners love the mild epithet, as it fits in with our moderate, even-keeled demeanor. If a White Midwesterner is teed off, he or she will likely abbreviate mild cuss words (such as p.o.'d or b-s) or, if especially upset, spell the offending word.

95. WHOLESALE CLUBS

Need a year's worth of toilet paper, 700 ibuprofen tablets, and 8,000 chicken nuggets? Look no farther than the White Midwestern wholesale club. Honest to Cher, you can't get outta the joint for under a hundred bucks. Oh, and you can pick up a new flat-screen TV and even eat enough free samples to feed a family of four. Plus, you can buy books there at a reasonable, discounted price (hint, hint).

96. ANTIDEPRESSANTS

You people think it's easy keeping up the famous stoic White Midwesterner façade? Oh glory, no—it takes a lot of work and a little bit of help from our friends at Eli Lilly and Company, the fine manufacturers of Prozac and other little life aids that help us get through the day without screaming at everyone in the Dairy Queen when they're out of Dilly Bars. (It's no coincidence that Eli Lilly is headquartered in the Midwest.)

Rx

Antidepressant

Fluoxetine Hydrochloride

50, 10mg. Tablets

97. POLKA FESTS

OK, I had to include this one for my aunt and uncle who are dedicated Wisconsin polkafesters. My uncle even plays the concertina, which is kind of like an accordion but less cool. Polka is really one of the few things from the old country that White Midwesterners have held onto. White Midwesterners don't care what you think about their polka fests, because they're too hopped up on cold beer, hot brats, and adrenaline to give a rip.

98. BOOK CLUBS

White Midwesterners love book clubs. I blame Oprah. No longer can you casually mention that you're reading a book without some well-meaning friend rapidly organizing a book club around it, complete with heavy hors d'oeuvres and wine, to meet at your house on Saturday afternoon.

99. EXPENSIVE PET CARE

In the olden days (the 1950s), companion animals got table scraps for food and weren't allowed in the house. This has all changed for the White Midwesterner, who showers more affection on the family pet than on any actual human being. Pets are White Midwesterners' emotional release valve in that way—without a way to release all that built-up ebullience, we'd likely explode. Hence the proliferation of big-box pet stores, where you can blow a paycheck on treats, leashes, doggy beds, and electronic litter boxes.

100. BEING OF GOOD HUMOR

White Midwesterners are gentle, kind people who don't usually get too bent out of shape over much and—most important—have the ability to laugh at ourselves. White Midwesterners are quick to laugh and tell jokes, and poke fun at ourselves just a little bit. What we may lack in sophistication we make up for in practical intelligence (you can keep Donald Trump, we've got Warren Buffett).

Photo Credits

All photos supplied from iStockphoto, except for:

1. RANCH DRESSING: Photo by Blake Stevens
2. BOB EVANS: Photo by Blake Stevens

11. HUGE CHRISTIAN CHURCHES: © JP Laffont/Sygma/Corbis

31. CHILD ONE-UPMANSHIP CAR ART: Photo by Caty Neis, with special thanks to Christine Schneier

54. CASEY'S GENERAL STORES: Photo by David Butler

63. WAL-MART: Photo by Blake Stevens

64. CRACKER BARREL: Photo by Blake Stevens

71. OLD-TIMEY PHOTOS: Thanks to models Kelly Hild and Scott Marsh

87. POTTERY BARN: Photo by Blake Stevens

I ♥ RANCH DRESSING